Ballads

Richard Owens

Ballads

Richard Owens

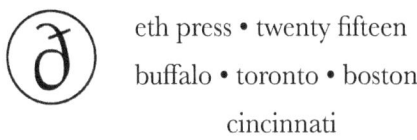

eth press • twenty fifteen
buffalo • toronto • boston
cincinnati

Ballads

Second edition published in 2015 by
eth press
an imprint of punctum books, Brooklyn, New York
ethpress.com | punctumbooks.com
(First edition published by habenicht press, 2012)

eth press is a parascholarly poetry press interested in publishing innovative poetry that is inspired by, adapted from, or otherwise inhabited by medieval texts.

eth press is an imprint of punctum books, an open-access and print-on-demand independent publisher dedicated to radically creative modes of intellectual inquiry and writing across a whimsical para-humanities assemblage.

Lisa Ampleman, David Hadbawnik, Chris Piuma, and Dan Remein are the editors of eth press, and we can be contacted at ethpress [at] gmail.com.

ISBN-10: 0615983936
ISBN-13: 978-0615983936

Library of Congress Cataloging-in-Publication Data is available from the Library of Congress.

This book was set in Walbaum type by David Hadbawnik.

Cover designed by Chris Piuma for eth press.

ACKNOWLEDGMENTS

The author extends heartfelt gratitude to the editors of the following journals, where some of the ballads included here previously appeared: *Big Bridge* (Dale Smith, guest ed.), *Blackbox Manifold* (Sam Ladkin and Robin Purves, guest eds.), *BlazeVOX* (Geoffrey Gatza), *Cambridge Literary Review* (Boris Jardine), *Kadar Koli* (David Hadbawnik), *Little Red Leaves* (Julia Drescher and CJ Martin), *Polis* (David Rich), *P-Queue* (Andrew Rippeon), *Poetry Wales* (Zöe Skoulding), *Pork* (Alessandro Porco), *Shearsman* (Tony Frazer), *Sous Les Pavés* (Micah Robbins), and *Veer About* (Will Rowe and Stephen Mooney).

For those objects included in the appendices, gratitude is due to the editors of *Skanky Possum* and *O Poss* (Dale Smith and Hoa Nguyen), Armen Chaparian of the Wretched Ones and Headache Records (Midland Park, NJ), Mark Noah of the Anti-Heroes and GMM Records (Atlanta, GA), Dim Records (Coburn, Germany), Knock-Out Records (Dinslaken, Germany), and TKO Records (San Francisco). Thanks also to Richard Parker of Crater Press for returning turncoat to itself.

PREFACE TO SECOND EDITION

Drummer boy quarters are not so present as they once were and I wonder now if we are not better for this. Mostly I see in these ballads what I believe might be the kernel of something redeemable—perhaps—even if this is only an enduring a priori energy spring-loaded into the source materials from which these romances depart and start again—and in this way they cannot but participate in processes of sedimentation and renewal—ongoing and unending—objects inclined to register the vestiges of lessons repeatedly learned and unlearned and so endlessly reformulated—what these here are—an anatomy and a grammar—of learning and unlearning, doing and undoing, repeating—as is—the ineradicable will of the form—an order—where no refrain is identical to anything other than itself in the instant of its dissemination—when activated by eyes and ears—and the continuities that keep these objects wired into one another also keep us grounded—like planes—restrained—to be engaged as demand and need determine.

Like the first edition, this second incarnation is dedicated to Michael Cross and Andrew Rippeon. Their Music. Their Labor. Additionally—along with those I have already thanked—I would like to extend deep gratitude to Orlando Reade, whose support for this work resulted in the 6 November 2013 symposium at Princeton focusing on this and the work of Tom Pickard, a poet whose writing has been close to me since I first read *Guttersnipe* in my Paterson, New Jersey apartment more than twenty years ago and whose *Ballad of Jamie Allen* is unquestionably the most significant and inspiring refashioning of the form since Helen Adam. The lion's share of my appreciation must go to friend, poet, scholar and comrade David Hadbawnik, without whose support these irremediably vulgar objects would have long since fallen out of circulation. Thanks are also due John Latta and Andrew Peart for their critical interest in this work, Meredith Martin, who participated in the Princeton symposium as scholarly respondent, and, somewhat more distantly, Susan Stewart, Dianne Dugaw, and Maureen McLane, whose research into balladry continues to inform my own sense of the liberatory possibilities latent within the practice.

Several of the weaker ballads which appeared in the earlier edition have been redacted while other instances have been appended.

Richard Owens
February–May 2015

CONTENTS

ACKNOWLEDGMENTS	vi
PREFACE	vii
BALLADS	11
WORKING NOTES ON BALLAD PRACTICE	111
APPENDIX I	117
APPENDIX II	124
APPENDIX III	131

WAYFARING STRANGER

tidings dost thou tether
ill will aerial bombings

marked from above
burly spear & brand

clamorous paean to place
ingratiate the local

diminutive—dull thud
do not remove the rubble

parse out a passive voice
in the present perfect

THY OLD CLOAKE ABOUT THEE

waxeth cold weather winter
gone down

blowes his blast—bold
put thine about thee

shoulders back to build

cover what is bare
to borrow to lend

true to the pale true to weare

cloth in grain
poor soule

take a new cloake about thee

IMMIGRANT SONG

mutual intelligibility—lonely time
weather wise roused
mine measured by a foreign model

frændr inhospitably near their own
throstle song hush—said grief
far inland from breakers dark frame

come to name wave upon shore
as before—light that lingers
still in the state of a whelping birth

tell me friend what ruin gives out
incongruent but salient worth
rushing with such shudder from seas

JOHNIE O COCKERSLEE

Braidhouplee—down in Bradyslee
for water to wash his hands

bound in iron bands—wolves
they again wyryeth women & men

manhuid shall fail me—sayed he
who war like called to his gud hounds

to marshal what news my man
speird sound—whisper pierced doun

dun deer feeding aneath a bush
this benison shall be o the very best

for mine—sayed he—courts lean
unweighted by pinch of the long haul

BONNIE SHIP THE DIAMOND

lackluster—lady for work
laying whiskey down

canned goods bottled goods
packaging presides

—sailors say
fetch another round

my life my lover my lady
—sea in passing

bear down bear away
loaded to the gunwales

—seized under rising tides
what a good wife you would be

FOREIGN LANDER

interminably blessed
merie sungen—heartland

genealogy thrust through the back

marks of distinction
fixed in a field of exclusion

remainder of an ancient lay:

embattlements—martial
trophies gathered
under the mantle of meaning

contour of a condition
salient countryside patria

MOTHERLESS CHILD

so little—added to the barrel
such a small thing
delicate call of its own landscape

winsome feet to be shoed
string to sound
through a little body—sometimes

the malt in the house we built
sits in a barn when
the ants go marching one by one

sometimes pigs are beat to eat
sometimes we feel
like a parking fine & away we run

BUNKER HILL

among the brave command
nominally under

captured positions
state of siege

pitched—immensity cloystered
iron wills to good

tamely fraile body
earthen redoubt

boost domestic spending
fructifie in mee

a refusal before advent
to control or contest

oedipal parricide
paradigmatic

stratagem—deceive
disavow or subvert

tend to the difference
reckoning

—grandstand fantasy
I conquered all my enemies

RIDE AN OLD PAINT

tails matted
backs raw

purchased
& tender

paid for
& stored

among the
old things

gathering they
cannot bear it

will not have it
—to be kept so

in the case
of having been

WABASH CANNONBALL

transpierced rounder gliding all
oblivious at length to advance
the jingle—the rumble—the roar

struck do strike iron straight rail
whosoever unknown raises
cosmologies of scale—rippling fall

indiscriminate on the first parable
crying out to all—waving
from the rapid Wabash Cannonball

MARCHING THROUGH GEORGIA

restrained from breaking boast
reckon with host reason fled

trumpeted—charge—given arms
shouted myth of manic death

suspended from a fig tree
aggregate Pharisees—sad splendor

an expanse habituates divinations
rat come to see—for itself

buried guilt gilded autumn
archangelic—like a shield left

strumming guttural stutter
still without a shape

built of stone—attention stood light
this was the edge of things

BONNY BARBARA ALLAN

o hooly hooly—gin ye be
on your death bed lying
so slowly aye as she put on
a garland for the dying

HUNTING OF THE CHEVIOT

sheep shudder in meadow
rustica—de res pastorelle
composed decoy to close in

on spectacular contending
ring & shake the rarest
then turn your head shining

being wrong forest & forage
sangis of the antiquite
an act of war—ecstatic you

ther cam an arrowe would
unbroken eyes vast rapt
on ether hand flying flocks

woefull hunting once there
to drive—encounter
mischance doth bleed by

distant dim call—billowing
power to wield moved
morningside sayd for shame

ROCK ISLAND LINE

watchdog howling (all caved in
beyond the pale—tis my home

cold wind implacable driven
unaccounted sooth shawl of sorrow

unplanned unmapped swallow order
blunt trees mended like man

even our shadows belabored in light
commonplace rumble—shaken

alliterative portrait of a ploughman
struck down cattle thief

contraband—pig iron—intermediate
between two states & cargo untold

undetected huckster amended airs
an untapped inventory—catholic

in the tall grass—laughing—mask
chimerical goods for summer sink in

TENNESSEE WHISKEY

—wipe the blood away
before I knock him off his chair

(into the courte is lighte
to resist—they took his hand

himselven—seemly by sight
fare by wood & echo down

like a fox on the run
busted flat—to knaw the cause

—down my last swallow
arrayed that commotion

(long ago & far away
called his children home

—let my secret go untold
branded—out in the cold

(that poor old wooden head
bound on a coach for cumly nighte

THE HOUSE CARPENTER

nettles—riverside
to scar the shins
they can feel the horses

hard hats—concrete
to pass the time
around the gorge

they want you raw
whitewashed—they go
phantasmagoric

bumpkins in reserve
trampled under spur
cold & naked

they want you broken
furrows drawn heavy
heavy colts suspended

compadre you want
to swap—hours for theirs
where water roars

flaxen hayseed—flesh
silver eyes pounding
the face of a landscape

DRUNKARDS SPECIAL

fearfull friends haunt this house
to collude—mortgaged land

wandered innocents
bargained with ruffians

(thy friends are all of hye degree
wrought a beneficial bane

sith I made thee my choice
quoth hee—between guns:

I don't like a railroad boss
incapacity to apprehend

& I of meane estate—full hard
daylight the old groom

innocents in the green
bad them straitwaye follow

running from the stable
pushed open the door—save

if thou bee taken under the gate
trace the strings upward in turn

OLD TOM OF BEDLAM

cut them down to size
pay them back in kind

with tools & tackles
furiouslye laid out

forth from our cell
for pity is not common

out of the compound
cocked & leveled

blind agency but could
turn into the yard

underpinning all of it
swallow to bleed

in an angrye moode
a small walled village

CHILDREN IN THE WOOD

dying charge departed from play
sore sicke—doleful—controlled

gimme a looke gimme a face
how deare—brought forth to light

from whence they take their place
falling to rise no more—buked

scorned—strike thine eyes
so the pretty speeche they had

now a vow to charge—die in armes
for executioners be made & oversee

OLD CHARIOT ALONG

that cross on Calvary
tossed & driven

city called Heaven
crown cast feet

sinner say—prophesy
commend de bones

(was a mighty back
I knowed gwine rise

sarpint quoiled round
ponstrous—for show

without pause or profit
—to catch the glint

gunned us stunned us
fo da money—foul

dayaam tenement shack
their whittles rubbed

pull—shadowes tow
de stone dem roll away

COMPLAINT FROM THE HOLY LAND

angelicke—nae mair she
(hath cleane forsaken me

knowe nor change
not the falling fruit

from his loins a likeness
to turn thee yet again

thro dun forest sacred dew
smiles upon a sacred bed

& by a lock of mine head
dare not lift mine eyes

revives—upon her feet
walking the cold walls

flame from flaring nostrils
sultry—forth into singing

my black eyed maid
behold—I also deal in fury

EZEKIEL SAW THE WHEEL

noisome beast to pass
out in the open field

nativity is the land
ceremonial benediction

thou hast built thy high
wheel run by faith

spoke was human kind
wherewith he fed thee

a high place in every street
delivered to cause

a parable unto the house
a great eagle with wings

cropped off the top—twig
clipped to become a vine

taken of the king's seed
that the kingdom be base

I shall eat coarser food
go worse—by various arts

to bring down the high tree
have exalted the low tree

NAKED IN THE DITCHES

phlegmatic on my bier
no regrets—my body bears
truth stem to stern
beginning with the hips

who am of common stock
looking to the sea
face ground—nothing now
conjured from dust

suffering—hung by the heels
sought occasion
as will was never conquered
to see the host broken

a swinging scythe—the dance
this most pleasant to me
so make moan for the old days
say why should love live

DARLING NELLIE GREY (MAGGIE MAY)

robbed sailors skinned whalers
cruising down the Canning Place
wake up Nellie—gadfly mute
restless in remorseless haste

amused & used at twa pound six
sleeping like it came to pass
tethered to his daddy's cue
where strangers fight to make it last

LES CLEFS DE LA PRISON

comen to this place—develich
(unable to stretch in the hold)

skies beclouded—triumphant
our dwellings pulled down

that by resoun the faithful fallyth
master or not—easily startled

crossed—like spars in a gale
retreat from roaring loud fellows

when softly a balmy wind blows
give ear—take luck pon water

clank upon air—buckle with
well harty—at home—call away

LAST OF THE FLOCK

lusty ewe fetched from rock
random guest—myself a guide

walk in law—defiled by way

they maketh me to lie down
for yielding pacifies offense

(were I not thus taught I should

catch from such wild banks
an account open to every heart

inhabiting the bosom of fools

GRANA WAIL (GRÁINNE NÍ MHÁILLE)

there came to me—fleecy garbs of gold and dun
a tower built (gown o covered in gore
stately hull a building high—shadow chair of state
parting friends a fit retreat) she wore

calm majesty—grave air—advisors by her side
iron chains clasped round her hands
(a wisdom in war—damsel fair—scarce represt
gilt—none her bearing) roving bands

brooch did bind—lo advance to certain kind
hail brine tears so pale & wan
come to greet—yield too far—rock built sea girt
eyrie—cut chord she rung refrain

destructive to trade—curious gaze—cast to sea
her plaintive wail shot through gale
gave galley to wind—her tresses fell unconfined
mid clouds came poor old Granuaile

BANKS OF THE OHIO

court my love so lily white
who dravest me headway

plunge (double penetration
over—qualified to advance

shatter the highest
(an exchange of currency

extrapolate from stats
the same everyday algebra

one man away from welfare
for we be so vicious withinne

lie snug (a soul demands ware
who seyde women loven best

same trade little esteemed
an irksome calculation

jolynesse—parcel ground
merely imaginary iron bar

only say repreve us oure vice
a natural particularity

in lieu of the main event
come with me & go—lest

CUMBERLAND GAP

lay down boys—take a nap
accommodate custom

bootstrap—family in twain
heave the blame herd

shatter cones in sandstone
ain no raf no mo—done

broke loose & gone
(how the pounding went on

anyways she's a goner
—come along with me boys

foller em (hear the axel turn
—cut tongue & trample

(an interest bore them down
—follow holler to catch

caught—unalloyed pleasure
splayed against stone

BORN TO RUN

round these velvet rims
on the street in a mist
pinch yourself—mask

or look at the banging man
banging back home
stitched in wasting flesh

where sun spends winter
(the way they fix his tie
full flowering—little doll

citizen—I feel myself
(this time spent without you
slipping down the road

sweet city woman—hold
like a country morning
unfamiliar as country rain

something sacred—a tune
them that got shall get
who got no bag or baggage

daylight discreetly muted
—how I'd like to fix his tie
all the hounds I do believe

please—hear me now
the show is over—we're alone
running back to you again

UNION BURYING GROUND

do not weep—quotidian
let the mourners come
made endeavor—sheer will

struggle sport upon shore
winding sheet wind
leave no single track behind

an assurance of security
out of line among
things that have no words

gnashing dirge—asunder
(integrated patterns of conflict
misread—never spoken

undone for duty done
bones—you alone in the dust
wrapped in linen—cold as clay

come anyhow with an offer
take delight in the dirty work
start—deal out the worst

superior industry standards
sewn into the earth
high frequency hardship—this

OLD COUNTRY STOMP

not my crime—not mine alone
heaven knows it of all things
could express carried accents

my faithful friend and servant
we set ourselves to serve
welcome the rod—our reason

poorly bread habit come patch
next day the same—bug
of wood in the road ways gained

linsey-woolsey—en it jist lovely
calmer thoughts to iron war
to attend the axe grace thy end

scattered strength makes the hearth
bedfellows consigned to sleep
they sass me in the holy gloom

SHACK BULLY HOLLER

roustabout—listen how it reads
four and twenty rowdy birds
well brass abrooud innermerica

wurnotjusst soshulism—rules
nor pitty warmes the preapproved
rocky mind naked about the rump

large bull—askance—hot muzzle
scratcheth bodies foule & faire
that owe we much to have throwne

strings or the odd tryst in care
tis fit—lefftoluvunderstate
law be arm to cry & does no good

git down anither throw away one
whistle post hove in sight
double decked highball stock car

out—crawled—have saw you fore
ef deys nachulborn tuzzle switch
done willed narrow in de bed yit

aincha come now chicken a mutton
flamdonies gwinter harness
like she rolls her doe to collar a nod

LOST AT THE COUNTY FAIR

to frenzy by grief night weareth old
feeds the canker oft but since

gars them all look sad—wark lifted
bitter days bridled like a horse

by way on the edge of the wilderness
short strictures conceal a sense

on the full of the moon—mean ways
ground out with a trenchspoon

stubbed—tainted—jostled to chase
suffered publick tumult

shimmering constraint—alike of earth
this system of truncated orders

how some wasn't even scared
undaunted by no one knew their names

BABA O'RILEY

tangled up in foreign hands
disband—this back into our living

unforgiven (loth themself to blame
crepuscular mind for mercy

shiver to hilt the proper way
riven—sway onward cross land

yonder view open plain to gain
unredeemed—stand to be bleed

mount again a stronger steed bare
check the rein—reign in

(apostolic in their own vile faith
beckoning—might well forbear

who thundering comes round
to scathe by brunt—the weight of it

advancing along the rocks
let us flee the face of this trembling

HENRY THE POACHER

you wicked & wily youth
companions beguile my ome

who know me well—betrayed
(pilots ferry supplies

freebase—to get some game
tripping along the pathway

faine methylbenzoylecgonine
they took us there by speed

like Job we stood with patience
accorded thore—tooke way

chainéd hand in hand
called to stray from land

there a gentleman took me
my master likes me well

black water—full four months
we ploughed the raging main

SHEPHERDS LAMENT

a good tree gives me shadow
pretty—behēoldon Þæt ęngel

koumfort wid she hann tek
de soffness—outwardly distant

tax-gatherers sent to scold
to meet & deal with us

messengers in their presence
embraced envoys—took stock

we were all very good friends
well disposed one to another

rapidly burning through reserves
for our part made no peace

having sewn such by such fed
quarterly losses—thence under

expected to match concessions
she stood turned to slip away

made me fast to assume cunning
tongue to the moving herd

now afield no longer standing
wræccan—with no hope of return

LEVEE CAMP HOLLER

darkened air silent loam
spare us to go back home

solemn debates below
a sacrificial extension

lilacs—your cross in rye
returning unquenched

traveling in good company
nourished by the mud

storm—cut into the music
hath risen to an occasion

public faces a yard long
drop shouts facing traffic

come round to collect
a plenty worth the getting

each found their own
gone far beyond the strand

THOMAS THE RHYMER

over fernie brae betide me weal
me woe—blude to the knee

braid braid road beset with thorns
weed-clotted marauding militia

disappeared—this for thy wages
synoptic scale low pressure storm

occluded—bosky den forest & fen
compacted in cheap triumph

outrun poorly minted blighted relic
thund'rous—cleave in twain

the weight of nimble necessity
touch & gild—hurry & go—bestow

fail to budge—the road—by grudge
toppling bales spanning ground

safe on second breathing spell
please—take your rest upon my knee

BENT SAE BROWN

gang and see tween my love & me
bauld sons I say gang & let us be
my love long tall—built for speed
he shout & cry my berry-brown steed

entreat win up get up off your feet
be my brand this goddamn town
my sweet baboo—am deeply sworn
aye you're a good man Sally Brown

for a kiss o your lovely mouth
auld sons way darna speak to thee
forbid us rest o north & south
broke your hame sae stole your me

LEESOME BRAND

what breeze proudly hastes
of an odd dawn
to draw on a market day

no—not the man I used to be
stronger underfoot
driven into dissimulation

two eyes offered to bandage
(bloom becomes you
this feast in your father's home

tis fair—that we lye there
croon large & wide
let fly these cudgeled memories

HONKY TONK ANGEL

ways & means—doing alright
sad women on low ground

my country girl moves me
screaming in the hallways

poppy blooms—skrotum
don't say much for syntax

some sort of capital rapport
variety of discombobulation

she's growing cold—a head
to pound on—a shiny egg

come with me—we'll go away
imagine a new locomotion

STEEL LAYING HOLLER

diminished resistance
sleeping on byways

in anny kase a gelding
—full liberty quoth

examine the work flow
observe local custom

polarized patterns of use
—magnetic metals

anything but accidents
manage narrow lanes

& who to lick our sores
this sack full of spurs

tractors bought at cost
—eviscerated colts

measured in horsepower
—graze on nostalgia

trace sweet muzzle & bit
headless trade winds

picking the rodeo clean
buck—gallop & break

traverse the course—see
no deviation from the mean

IROQUOIS STEEPLECHASE

this wicked gallon of rye
when a man loseth
in his commodity for want

take like recompense dear
by providence
where there is scarcity for

for now is the hand of God
upon the commodity
infuriated by the light sum

of man—common coasters
unprofitable fowlers
armigerous families forsooth

more calibrated than colored
beyond yon weari hand
vast forces variously at war

saints deep in their ecstasies
wrassle to extricate
thousands of fencible goods

outward piety & inward purity
subdivided ad infinitum
like some kind of wild scripture

EL ABANDONADO

me abandonastes—near the public road
or the stars across the way
copper or tin—a bellwether calls me home

these Albuquerque kisses—near misses
or a fella needs a car
to call on the bright tin women & pitches

figs & oranges from the more mature trees
or your mother is watching
from the caboose of an old military train

RETURN OF DJANGO (IVANHOE RHYGING)

wreck a pum pum—his hands
are completely broken

can you hear this—gypsy
manouche—cascading

arpeggios—broken chords
caravan to disinterred clouds

shottas—Django shoots first
shantytown tempo di massacro

dis bamba clot chop di wood
such a hard man wanted fe dead

JOHN THE REVELATOR

an advocator—bot wi blude
bound for some
what shortly comes to pass

companion through affliction
as of a trumpet
who was detained among you

for their power is in the open
between hands
an indivisible wilderness

idol clothed in precious raiment
waiting in glory
a fire come on thee as a thief

a nakedness kept from the hour
come & see
deep in the rocks of mountains

that hath an ear let them hear
these against thee
world to rent—a living so bent

ROCKING CHAIR MONEY

worries & fears—sure—so called
tipping sights for a straightened gait
a cardinal question—capital gains

rollover advection feedback
contribution limits—so solid & still
saved money measured earnings

an assortment of mutual funds
that changed the lock on our front door
so much better than no house at all

but we done let the deal go down
clear—collectivized investment pools
ordinary factory farms—associate

incentives—kolkhozy—an open
ended stampede circling assets invested
beyond the limit of taxable events

a list of deferred compensations
a hole in our bucket—an option to buy
such stable risks that never return

SWEET HOME ALABAMA

will remember—southland shoals
spilling swampland black belt

river shallowing southward
gravel—silt—cobble—shingle

will remember—tidal flats
water gates natural dams big wheels

beaten down in honor to promote
sedimentary herringbone structures

GREAT SPECKLED BIRD

despised by the squad
mine heritage assembles me

in this bour dwelling
to devour come what day

say by & by—by & by
beasts of the harvest field

round about against her
saying peace when there is

shame in ways—stumbling
my hand upon inhabitants

full of days on the wings
blush—her name is recorded

COCAINE BLUES

down just about midnight
all the angels
rapt—what—to fetch out

thrilled in skinned brass
calling him home
built on edge—still at ease

up with his old sweetheart
& I ran laughing
home before the landlord

she knew—how to move
ain't never seen her
hustle the same run twice

FOGGY MOUNTAIN BREAKDOWN

nervous conditions conturbat me
mounted bey der hand
despoiled planks of the aviation

ascend disembodied—unaccounted
costs earmarked for sidelines
settled into states cut off from tribes

compared & ranked insofar as use
neurologically grounded
raises what holy ritual from the hills

SWEET LADY JANE

you give you give
smile you give
marked by a light

faint single mouth
fade to dim
where the clouds

face away the field
rest in dark
far echo to stand

moisten your lips
pause to land
afraid it all began

OTHER SIDE OF TOWN

meet me on the corner—to spare
(some say) den live opprest

the need here always for more
who don't live around

them blow—dust & ashes long ago

they teach at ease
these termes fit for the Devill

cast away when we came late

convinceing returne none the lesse
run ourself to death

at every turn—afeard of the road
crosse to foreine soyle

TIE SHUFFLING CHANT

ears ope wide—jaw the team
they cannot ride

(blindside turtle ditch

legal—tender—the flesh
granted to claim difficult ways

uninsured—no wayes carefull
employed about

unhandsome work—to assist
mistake our interest

(inasmuch as they were people

glossing over several points
plotted to map

we were cold then—we read
fully restrained

to have such credit with Thee
further to extend

(inscribed upon these very feet

POOR MAN LAZARUS

his wounded side tells naught
but defies by bonds
the high sheriff or hanging tree

debtor in possession—troubled
project financing
buy back settlement spinoffs

to our relief—we are not willing
to be bondsmen
never at our own cost—gardens

thrust back into the common gaol
which is all at present
what you owe & refuse to yield

HOMEWARD BOUND

when I was a young boy
we ran dog & bell—lingering windes
cut down ancient codes
outward—for these were the worlds

unavailable exit strategies
wastefully conceded to make sense
in economic doldrums
struck through with an old embrace

divine force stood waiting
responsive to our dire need to escape
to another place—there
to avail a defiant share sweeping eyes

COLUMBUS STOCKADE

turned as we lay sleeping—our antiquities
sent their herald with a letter
harvesting new centers—they too turned

from Genoa—followed by atrophy still
some distance from headway
unblinking as I believe they fought against

too many mornings to waste a good deal
their effect grossly mistaken
for the ludic rest of a murtherous wildness

LES MARINS DE GUERRE

not the smooth ways polite & cold
pull with a will—rumbelow
undercut the volatility of work at flow
domiciled some time ago

heave away—disembark having round
that old uneasy conviction
hauled away to grind a thought to pass
a dire strait or erring predilection

SAIDE TO HIS MAMMY

racke to back a kindness til they tired
the broken cold don't envy me
but pity the limits—better for to tarry

disguise our unshieldedness that this
so familiar fades—what
changing breast held against lesser shades

ONCE THRESHING WHEAT

split properties—our calaboose
(living labor time kicks
all those lives so to tow the heart

tethered to a moonlit apparatus
passing beneath the frame
of a rhyme for the same old same

BORDER CATTLE THIEF

regrettable loss of butchered kine
contradicts its character
midst mild spoke endemic increase

ride hard on capacities for abandon
torn loose from we build
settlements in a comforting nostalgia

subdue the disease constitutive of
we cannot move today
or be restless till warm weather comes

who never settle down to the task
but snatch it from behind
insist on the security of spot price stock

MAY DAY CAROL

we bring you a branch of May
budding out against September

with the disturbance of spring
distempered—at the heart

plies the stone apart then goes
into the dark—interstellar

vacancies offer unimagined
recourse to action—an applied

physics built on a shaky surface
that offers no secure purchase

claim yourself a branch of May
to line your living well within

TULLOCHGORUM

like ole philosophorum
cut down these crops

they ascend in steady sun
or tender a long march

flesh out the heaving chest
coral the salvages

crowd out dynamic scoring
flag down the barmaid

disconsolate—run to the tap
go hold out your glass

BELLE OF BATON ROUGE

little girl—tree among trees
settled below
the clean coils of a rich thicket

of all the whorish crews
encounter
none—but cowards by mast

to avert their shining eyes
go laughing
precise—length of a coffin

land over at the loading dock
to die now
marshaled—such sprite lumber

last nail driven immaculate to
forward with
to be—replaced & so quietly lay

gently rocking to final rest
a cold expanse
buckled gangplank of the town

CARRICKNABAUNA

hoist melodius musicke—pleasant roundelaies
fit out a good barque as it fell on a holy day
ambling nag—spouting & sporting—trow it be

for only the breadth of a farthen cut the curtain
split the seams—what bayberry kame glashet
for both a crowning courage a canon plide roaring

COMPLEATE GENTLE WOMAN

each creature in all respects unfolds aright
(dainty sweets found deare—without defense
as alms turn us toward an unstable hearth

to freeze by fire side without a curbing bit
our unfolding bitterness unbridled—unleashed
lassitudes to aggravate the welladay fog

scrape the cables grease the wagons wish
we was dead to serve the grieving heart sore
an empty milking pail or luckless chance

these rural words bewail what never comes
by mail but might be made from small beades
disposed perhaps of the power to pardon

sufficient to convey the whole—quietly
to traffick in the qualitie of a terrible mistake
provided we ride through a gentle assembly

GREENFIELDS OF FRANCE

how do you do—without a name
emblazoned on poor housing projects
extended to a state of emergency

what mosque in Saint-Chamond
fire bombed—as if they had a part
(to all things their leaf assigned

such running an almost normal
situation—an ugly race whose lips
are so fat they hiss with no tongue

Clichy-sous-Bois—another isle
where thy Cross is common wood
without our good meat to bear

nevertheless a people live there
in power substations—across the grid
& for wickedness suffer such shock

HAUL AWAY JOE

towed away frames from the fat on down
spoiled his constitution—poor soul
no flesh no bone but a mask far worse
than ten deaths waiving their right to hold

a simple juridical observance remarking
this dismemberment toward the state
unwilling he represents the necessary proof
of an abandonment fueled for shame

I work says he to keep the good ship rolling
a commonly adopted—mode of action
he is so much more his own peculiar person
an accustomed half getting no satisfaction

UNDER THE GREEN WOOD TREE

converge—birds see no enemy
whatever rough weather
marks out the landscape—spread
in all directions or in a bird's

molting feathers watch disease
undercut sweet song so
all fish have their net—regret
reconfigured in struggle

how harsh praise offered against
inadequate endeavor sounds
cosmetic—or under a tree—crawl
haul away from our own good

BATTLE OF BULL RUN

variable constituent—that awful rebel yell
how she lay in the willows dead

movement becomes crucial—demands
mechanisms & the circulating

contour of a cosmopolis—to begin with
or the bitter crises that emerge

by way of an overconsumption that strikes
the libido down—we belong

upon the face of the earth but for a mo-
ment
mein kinder gaze in wonder

their way was not a road so we fell down
through a fissure in the image

they walled us up in mountains—warned us
for if we make the least noise

we foolishly disclose the way to these wings
but living so far below the surface

even when our face is dirty we must decide
or resign to take them by surprise

NORTH TO ALASKA

from the claws of a bear
our friends feared
we might encounter more

& they came to a point
—an opening
that carried the great beast

we are in their country
taken away
watching the wooden folks

undo the hinges of wings
to store them
until they wake us up again

CHALKDUST FAREWELL

called back slaves bound down
—less than blest—tis help to live
occupied in chutes picking slate

din of arms inserted heretofore
mindest thy duty—do well to give
the best of every masked conceit

while clinics of the whole diversify
species into niches—who captive
take to black chalk or crushed ashes

beneath the arc of fulsome skies
mines allegorize such a wild abyss
lost like the ground beneath living

IN MY OWN SHIRE

if they was sad rue we bore
—this honorable gift
struck year by year to remain

a team to plough betrays
—power on power
so steeped in truceless light

confide in like conditions
—profligate divisions
wedged within what systems

charge this natural basis
—for their work
advancing unsettled agendas

pretenders guide us round
—to have our bones
planted by force in solariums

BLIND CHILD'S PRAYER

act like trash—leave be large
until then no fantasy
fall all to admire—no use now

how the most was being framed
ground down to a halt
cause the house was greater still

master deck managed well
gone tailor to rig
stuck behind the wheel—anneal

the crude steel under the hood
cutting up the road
how we in our wake brave away

AMERICAN GIRL

a little more to life—alright
then you are good
refined in me worthiest thing

how low you lay under praise
in the dark hour
sudden care to know then dare

in the dark light—what might
put our temples
down without our due discretion

the impression a good girl leaves
in wake yet hence
no recompense for what way goes

SALLEY GARDENS

perverse sex outside agender
—this transistor radio
truth value blasted a go go
—well worn to bend her

hostile stares mock to face
—a recondite disgrace
else cure his traitorous gait
—with a wholesome balm

encompassing no continuum
—for his mistress he prays
solid state to snake in repose
—carry go bring me this venom

EARLY ONE MORNING

hazard ruine—combustion all sides round
they do not deceive in the valley below
when overwhelmed by the deluge they fall
from sense to skies beating like hearts

till then who knew grace could offer up all
burning offal against ceiling cracks
with adverse power opposed—yield unto
a fixt sum masking settlement patterns

stopping at a well to rest—durst dislike
but settle for a place so far afield
stunned by an unconquerable acquaintance
squarely at the center of this cadence

so it beats—blown away by redacted light
how people feed themselves at night
can else inform the blind force of token arms
scouring settled land for branch or bone

DAYBREAK BLUES

an account told or enacted
—tooled into an absence
on the finest milling machine

tomorrow belongs retooled
take the dirt road home
meet undiminisht what untold

to avail though forget we feel
often an instance to grieve
do deceive under sovereign pact

four at the foot six at the head
suffer a surface like blood
burned before us by permission

we belong to an ordered design
scaly rind—enraged
but serving well to bring forth

forthwith the backward slope
in billows blind by right
we run with force for morn delay

DOWN BY THE RIVERSIDE

study my burden—no more
whom serving hath made
greater—in my choyce to see

if for once in worst extream
pursued by thir rowling
we turned away from the wake

then all might be nonesuch
floating carkases strewn
pushed to swelling beyond us

we move in abject posture
(they mean us to fight
crumbling heroic constrictor

whom they no longer respect
but crawl where we stood
strapped to the heavenly record

BLOW OUT THE CANDLES

then when you were apprenticed
on fertile banks—intrencht

bright eyes for decorative padding
the brisk set turned

enhanced there by stately growth
down—cast—damp

witnessed all the more come through
standing like but against

repulsed—assayed in spite of scorn
lest our noise too bar the door

DOWN THE HATCH

blow my bully boys
clear away
unanswerable style

squared summons
dropt—rout
an all access throng

suffer no hat tricks
lout roll out
by charge of sound

insufferable light
so numbered
below—unsupported

blow out—seaward
wan pale course
fairly measured specs

THERE USED TO BE A BALLPARK

where the kids ate cotton candy
right here—do you mind
if I rest for a spell by this stone
alone or obscene when they
lowered you down—well done

no doubt there was only a future
advantages for everyone
our only support against pushing
some confused base—hit
thrown into an anticipated coming

RAIN ON THE SCARECROW

four hundred empty acres somehow made right
dangle overhead on strictly speaking
disentanglements offsetting gossamer forbearance
rent among fitful threads laid bare

in the cupboard of unforeseeable opportunities
disordered by the rowdiest tame under will
blood invites an endowment for just such a past
slack jawed—fluently scorched—blight

UNEMPLOYMENT STOMP

our meal was in our field
—hunger itself
probably more than mine
unseen—whose

name in an earlier way
meant potential
for new meat hung to dry
in old smokehouses

CROOKED TRAIL TO HOLBROOK

intolerable prattle—bid farewell—to the cattle
eating prairie hay wounded from lip to hip
—silvern chatter derogations dismissed as before
wise or unhurried—smoothly unanswered

what plucked at least for them low hanging fruit
blossoming out of hand on petroleum fueled trinkets
to mount thoughts that shake the scaffold loose
—all reasonable things flee unstable embattlements

but residual pulp confounds our ability to perform
thoroughgoing risk assessments—these barren pastures
unregistered in the bruit or mistaken for the plenty
to which we carry nonplussed selves—heavy—to graze

raze the charred land—split it down the middle
or recognize our fear indeed suffers no wild flowers
stirred to life on the trail between tracks
that tremble under the incontinent law of their ground

TANGLEWOOD SWAMP

brackish entirely to way—by prime of day
we understand our worthiness

their counsel to play time till we're gone
riding fealty—sudden command

or that one there to proffer us wrong
yet—now it is—so openly

abiding analyses held down by the name
with more than many may do

—well here is our body to make it good
departing from pleasaunce

refugees of—low lying—last resort under
foot stand unique among drainage

basins—though the fish were never quite fish
nor the waterfowl domestic at all

HOUSE OF SAD RETREAT

floating rates of exchange remainder
next of kin—an occasion

intensified thereafter—an internal
policy—this act of union

fathom stroud waters convey the whole
—bargaine among thieves

stable reserves—currencies desaturated
by law—so prepared all treasons

administered justice—fast misprisions
—felonys—seditions—calumnys

bullbaiting—cockfighting—bear beating
contract out the public house

IN THE UPPER ROOM

through tall grasses
between these names
& dates & battles
darkness comes early

forrotian—uneasy
passing wi gude will
improved means
to an undiminished end

it was never unclear
these—years trusting
a pace of approval
twisted into bold rings

distinctions between
malign capacities—must
—as ever—be rigidly
oþ—dweller—observed

NEVER WALK ALONE

courteously together as frames upon pain
without a stitch or timely word
beaten & thrown—walk on—headlong gone

bryght futures so about sold catch hem reste
feasts spread across heaving breasts
said then: the sun hath song in sorrow's waste

JOANNIE WORKS WITH ONE HAMMER

then—she goes to sleep
glaidly to thoill
n qhua is they hounggrie

when they work with two
devastated
by the frost—taken to raise

greit mercie on principle
to lend—drains
gude work instrumental to

three hammers simmer
in the hole
overnight hotter than coal

orchards link directly to
four hammers
quhais power is nocht theys

secured—in the pit—for
their fude they work
with five when then to sleep

TAKE ME BACK HOME

not long—before the war
among children
these godley sportes to pass

for the razors
were ever wonder

in the night—like them pigs
can sing maybe they fly

away from this
say so long right

never—too late—coming up
to killit us—now & agin

who will be
returned—repeated

turn us loose—let us go
cowering how
crying—taken so from the till

BLACK MOUNTAIN RAG

to cling to—smash—smallest thane
burnished chance to spill
bereaved so kind of a common world

out there in the dark—we poor thing
where were we all night
who could at least come back for good

on these poor legs—taken round
long—into the black
lashing blind at rock & thicket flung

och skammen—affection is so often
an unyielding thing
maligned by a far more available fruit

MAGGIE LAUDER

well met—bladderskate—scornful to my trade
shake a leg—wallop over the field
break long ways—from—key performance indicators

down at the base—research & regnal hymns
collected round campfires
burn white at the aggregate limit of impact factors

SWEET DARLING

these untuned hues—configured—to play
in morning light the mile
walked—side wise—fine shadows trashed

footsteps ground large—set—for begging
terror bestride uncarved calls
with love driven to build a rapt summer stair

an incomplete moment lost to the straight
ways bridled round wise
decisions—locked—faintly remembered back

apart from rote prayer plundered for gone
advance of stays fooled
to bloom by—wise—restricted mass of days

I hear you—hallway bound—walking sound
grown dear in the dim light
blunted—treasured against our inability to know

WAR ON THE STREETS

tonight—mired in the maelstrom
covered in mud
out with the noise—alright—settled

into old scores locked tight tonight
conspired—blindside
waged against a cabined community

in a useless heap formed under law
fell flat on the floor
to feel small understanding nothing

BILLY IN THE DARBIES

his marrowbones shackled out
(ignore paraphenomena
patterned winds—cycloid—smile

through the trauma in their hearts
(auguries sound this hour
so sleep fathoms deep—slake notes

crossing unsurveyed surfaces
(greasy hogs brood
on the collateral organs of others

muted—signal bright derivations
(disendowed questions or
the congratulated weight of tongues

OFTEN WHEN WARRING

bespoken—thuswise hustled
wired through juvenile platitudes

unprotected against
outperforming muscularities

a permissible rage—tendering
no wise—defenestration

among friends—friendly officers
attend to the bleakest of species

dragged willingly across
the scorched earth of having been

an instrument—to get us through the brush
this guaranteed hush—this bore to take
coiled—who resolutely lie awake—in sense
to mend sense—a space—far too willing

WORKING NOTES ON BALLAD PRACTICE

I. *THE MAST*

The species of an eye with the neck of an owl—a circumspect specimen that carefully considers the conditions of an outcome. Respectus. The act of looking round or back, to regard or attend to with eyes. The act of looking backwards with an eye that aspires to behold the whole so that when J.H. Prynne speaks of respect it is in the interest of fresh light—of reviewing what the eyes have already seen, a music previously muted by shadows:

> Since I crossed the sea just like a ballad, with the one guarded hope, to give you this as a totally specific gesture: a respect which runs out into time like light.

So he says to Olson, redirecting his gaze, running out. There is no deference here. Only the care of eyes for the potentialities of a buried music. Like Odysseus lashed to the mast—or more appropriately, Marina's father moving across an oceanic expanse:

> His kingly hands, haling ropes;
> And, clasping to the mast, endured a sea
> That almost burst the deck.

Shakespeare's *Pericles*—where the ropes that secure sails to masts and ensure good voyage vibrate like the chords of a throat. And the pressures brought to bear on the deck are no different than the altitudes and depths that push the drum of an ear near to the point of rupture. The mast that thrusts up from the deck is where we assemble.

II. *THE FIRE*

Like sound and sense ballads circulate. And it is the circulation of air that creates the conditions for fire. Too often paper beats rock—but only so long as it stays in circulation, reified, away from the movement of the burning flames that call our attention to time. And if there is any one collection of ballads that most worked to retard the perishing instant of fire it is Thomas Percy's 1765 *Reliques of Ancient English Poetry*. Published in three volumes, the collection is built around a seventeenth century manuscript and intended, Percy says, "to inquire by what gradations barbarity was civilized, grossness refined, and ignorance instructed." Although Percy's *Reliques* enjoyed a wide and enthusiastic readership that included Wordsworth and Coleridge, the "ancient" folio manuscript upon which it was built remained in the possession of the Percy family and unavailable to readers for a century until, at Francis James Child's behest, F.J. Furnivall and John W. Hales retrieved it from Percy's descendants and prepared it for formal publication in 1868. Brought out in four volumes as *Bishop Percy's Folio Manuscript*, an opening essay contained in the second volume offers an account of the circumstances surrounding Percy's acquisition of the manuscript. Here Furnivall and Hales quote from a note inscribed by Percy in the manuscript itself:

> This very curious old MS. In its present mutilated state, but unbound and sadly torn, I rescued from destruction, and begged at the hands of my worthy friend Humphrey Pitt, Esq. then living at Shiffnal in Shropshire, afterwards of Prior Lee near that town; who died very late at Bath; viz. in Summer 1769. I saw it lying dirty on the floor under a bureau in ye Parlour: being used by maids to light the fire.

Ignorance is instructed when unlettered, untutored servants are taught the error of their ways. Or a culture's past becomes the infancy of its present when songs are rescued from children accused of mishandling the objects of their labor. But there are fires to build. And few know better than a servant the value of warmth and light generated by flame in a moment of bitter darkness.

III. *THE MUSIC*

Children love songs and in fact make them—but music

properly belongs to adults. Adults are the guardians of children and their custody naturally extends to anything a child might make. In other words, employees that produce anything on company time know in advance these objects properly belong to the company. But 401(K) investment plans offer employees the illusion of ownership, suggesting workers are no longer employees but associates that now have a personal stake in the success of the companies they labor for. Apropos: the following passages from a recent exchange with Andrew Rippeon concerning lyric practice:

> AR: Lyrical as an adjective, applied to the currency of popular song forms? As if popular song forms aren't innately also lyrical? Lyrical as nothing without a direct object to modify? And I remember here Wordsworth in either his Advertisement, Preface, or Afterward to the *Ballads,* writing that he chooses rude or common life because invention and idiom (cult of "the new...") are often mistaken for truly elevated experience—he calls the affectation of idiom the "hubbub of words." So it seems like WW is trying to reduce the experiment (and I do think WW is experimental *precisely* in the degree to which he mobilizes folk forms, attempts various forms of empathy, and considers his use and circulation of the currency of metrical patterns...) to the lowest common denominator, to cut out Shelleyean whim and explore what remains as the possibility of lyricism.
>
> RO: Thinking about Wordsworth and the mobilization of folk forms—that the ballad as form needs a qualifier in order to somehow recuperate or revitalize it, like the coronation of a peasant—man, my jerking knee coughs up Ives (selling insurance against the wrong disaster). In Wordsworth the modifier serves to elevate, right? I mean, everyone has an idea they know what a ballad is. It's this degraded thing shot through with a sense of pastness, cultural infancy and a charming but sometimes dangerous rusticity that needs to be carefully framed and reined. In the case of Wordsworth, his appeal to ballad practice—and lyric—is, like you say, considerably more complicated. In most cases ballads are nothing more than vehicles hijacked or manufactured to map

> a desired past onto the poverty next door—a sort of slumming that brings the black sheep of the family to the funeral that never ends. I mean, ballads are those angelic whores from the other side of town that rich men sometimes marry—but only in fairy tales (the appeal to gender is essential).

Women and children. In the cultural imaginary women are children. Like any good woman, children are pure. They are said to be what we were before the collapse, unsullied by knowing better or knowing at all. Forms are assigned to these children and sirens are the women Odysseus must delight in without being seduced by their song. He knows better.

Nor can we know how many ballads trickled down to common people from court poets through a specifically cultural form of supply-side economics. Wyatt was a poet of Henry's court when he wrote: "Ye must now serve to market and to faire, | All for the burden for pannyers a paire."

Or a culture's modest past becomes the infancy of its wealthy present when children are accused of making the objects rescued through the labor of adults. Adults often play the role of rescue workers that pull bodies from under the rubble of collapse, not so much to save them but rather to preserve and memorialize. Ann Yearsley, the milkmaid of Bristol, is said to have been rescued by Hannah More. But children often know well what is worth rescuing, even when they themselves are the object of rescue. More importantly, they know what is properly theirs. If it is not theirs they actively make it their own, mutilating and defacing the objects in their possession until they can one day be restored and preserved again by adults.

Guthrie and Leadbelly often performed for children and some critics have even called attention to their child-like qualities. Here one can reasonably assume that for an adult like Robert Southey both Guthrie and Leadbelly would have been—as Stephen Duck or John Taylor were—ideal specimens of untutored genius. They certainly were for Alan Lomax. On the other hand, Bascom Lamar Lunsford—esquire, to be sure—was known to travel dozens of miles on foot through the southern Appalachians of North Carolina to collect the ballads of the people he so loved. Something like a father picking up after his children. And children are never to be trusted with large sums of money—or anything more than what they immediately need to satisfy baser but permissible appetites. Adults handle capital. But servants often know well when to start fires and what to fuel them with.

IV. *THE WAR*

Chanson polemique. In the ancient sense polemic—the polemical—is war and the internal contradictions at play within the frame of any ballad make of each a protracted conflict often violently disarticulated from the processes that keep them alive. Like any order of song, ballads are sites of struggle; their production and reproduction are interventions, willful or otherwise, in that struggle.

Music properly belongs to Apollo not Dionysus. Ian Hamilton Finlay knew this well when he had inscribed across the façade of his cottage home: HIS MUSIC | HIS MISSLES | HIS MUSES. Chilean soldiers knew this well when they broke the hands of Victor Jara, threw down a guitar and asked him to play.

V. *THE PATHOS*

Per the Greek suffering and experience are one and the same: pathos. But on the terrain of classical rhetoric pathos is neither suffering nor experience as such and is instead a species of persuasion that reproduces experience in order to carry one capable of decision or intervention into a certain condition. It is never more than one component of a much larger whole, a part among parts integrated in an overdetermined complex of ongoing processes. But it is precisely this part that moves one to give the shirt off their back against the better jury of our reason. And this can only be the work of pathological liars or what lies through the grace of a lyre—a set of strings signaling the coordinates of a distant situation. It is not the whole of a situation but a distress signal that simultaneously sounds and responds to a situation. And depending on their situatedness such signals either challenge or act in accord with other parts embedded in the whole; or like pharmakoi these signals move as slaves among criminals, heroes among rescue workers, whores among men; they are both the cause and the cure, the ochlos—at one and the same time the people and the rabble; they are the ground any successful democracy wholly depends on, wholly produces, publicly celebrates and secretly despises. These signals are the mast we assemble around.

APPENDIX I: THOSE UNKNOWN
PREFATORY NOTE

From 1988 through 1997—a full decade—I performed with my brother, Bill Owens, in Those Unknown, the first decidedly socialist Oi! band in the US. In this we followed founder of Oi! Records, Roddy Moreno of the Oppressed, who insisted: "Oi! = A WORKING CLASS PROTEST (NOTHING MORE—NOTHING LESS)." While the masculinist underpinnings of our grasp of class struggle at that time obviously inhibited our ability to fully articulate the concerns that most troubled us with other struggles, these underpinnings offered us a generative point of departure for what I believe has been a lifelong inquiry into working class masculinity and the role it plays in the social reproduction of capital as an unimpeachable socioeconomic phenomenon. And having played drums—having been committed to the practice of beating percussive objects—I am now reminded of the colonial drummer on the 1976 bicentennial quarter designed by United States Mint engraver Frank Gasparro. This would be labor.

In an essay dedicated to DC-based poet and activist Gaston Neal (1934-1999), Amiri Baraka writes, "The Word is the FIRST DRUM." Below this he then writes, "The Drum then Follows." This is contradiction—generative contradiction—such that the drum which comes first follows. This is a listening. At once the first to arrive and the last to leave. For this to be so the drum as object must listen. Here the word as the first drum must listen; it is thus that language designates not a speaking but a listening. And so I listen to others—Dale Smith, Sean Bonney, David Grundy, others—they calling me back to Baraka who lived on South 10th Street in Newark—just one street over from where my father was raised. This matters. This is contradiction. And in his brief 1984 commentary on Bruce Springsteen, Baraka writes:

> Would perhaps that there were more American youth independent of the double maw of working-class economic insecurity and lack of education (hence, often, political sophistication) to be as clear as Springsteen on what being born in the USA, for instance, yokes a young white (and black) working-class youth to.

This then would be the task and continued labor of ballad building. Perhaps. This.

DISCOGRAPHY

A. ELAPSED PLAY

Those Unknown. 7" ep. 33rpm. Midland Park, NJ: Headache Records, 1991.

Going Strong. 7" ep. 33rpm. Midland Park, NJ: Headache Records, 1992.

Distribution. 7" ep. 45rpm. Sussex, NJ: Pogostick Records, 1995.

B. FULL-LENGTH LP

Those Unknown. CD. Atlanta, GA: GMM Records 1995.

Those Unknown. LP. 33rpm. Dinslaken, Germany: Knock Out Records, 1995.

Scraps. CD. San Francisco, CA: TKO Records, 2003.

Those Unknown. CD. San Francisco, CA: TKO Records, 2003.

C. OMNIBUS ENDEAVORS

The Only Spirit is Unity. 12" LP. Coburg, Germany: Dim Records, 1993.

American Headaches, 2. CD. Coburg, Germany: Dim Records, 1994.

Backstreets of American Oi!: Unreleased Anthems. CD. New York, NY: Sta Press Records, 1994.

The United States of Oi, 2. CD. Atlanta, GA: GMM Records, 1995.

RASH (Red and Anarchist Skinheads) Anthems: Fighting Music for the Working Class. Cassette. New York, NY: RASH NYC, 1997.

SHREDS: 5 (The Early 1990s). CD. Hoboken, NJ: Shredder Records, 1997.

Limited Options Sold as Noble Endeavors: Benefit Compilation. 10" EP. Minneapolis, MN: Half-Mast Recording Corporation, 1997.

Punch Drunk III. CD. San Francisco, CA: TKO Records, 2001.

Punch Drunk IV. CD. San Francisco, CA: TKO Records, 2002.

With the exception of a word here or a phrase there, and some minor involvement in developing arrangements, each specimen below written and composed by Bill Owens.

INSTANCES

i. NO RHYME NO REASON

There was once was a playground
Where the children used to play
And there once was a factory
Where there fathers worked through the day
But now in its place
Stands the proof of capitalist gain
So whose to say that
Everything will be okay?

Soon it came to pass
That the children played no more
And their fathers in the factory
Couldn't accept the reforms
Of longer hours of work
And a decrease in the rate of pay
No longer are they needed
So they're gonna throw them away.

It was said it couldn't be
But they brought us to our knees
And we said if this ever happened
We would fight
Now we're living off our past
And we're living off our dreams
I'm not gonna take it; I really really hate it
I'm not gonna make it; So I'm gonna fight.

The children soon grew old
Only to take their fathers' place
In another time and another land
To fill an old man's space

No longer shall they search
For the golden light
Cause the future's just a daydream
And tomorrow's just a fright.

[Sussex Co. NJ 1991]

ii. THE ANSWER

All this time I lived a simple life
No nothing too extreme
& I told myself as a frightened little child
Gonna grow up and be something
But now my childhood's over
And what remains from those scenes
It's a question seeking an answer
What happened to my dreams?

I tried to find the answer & found nothing to believe
I was told to keep my chin up—for what?
So they can kick me in the teeth
The question still remains but one thing's crystal clear
I gotta keep plugging to get ahead around here

Try to stop it now
Try to figure it out
Try to stop it now
It'll never ever, never ever, never ever bring me down.

You tried to find the answer and found nothing to believe
You were told to keep your chin up—for what?
So they can kick you in the teeth
The question still remains but one thing's crystal clear
You gotta keep plugging to get your ass outta here.

Now you listen to their bullshit
Ring, ring goes the bell
They give you ten fucking minutes
To smoke a couple cigarettes

& then it's back to your cell
Well you could have had your own office
& all your childhood dreams
But now it's 5:30 go to work
Think yourself a fucking jerk
Who never ever learned anything

You tried to find the answer and you found nothing to believe
So you went to work for a year or two
& said this will solve everything
Now time has passed you by and one thing's perfectly clear
Sometimes you're looking for an answer you don't want to hear.

[Sussex Co. NJ 1991]

iii. DARKER HOURS

There's a trap door in any pocket you'll find
Mine's been sprung quite some many times.
They can take away our homes and throw away our lives
& wonder why we're so down.
Don't you worry I won't be patronized
Someday soon we'll kick them right between the eyes.

But for now there will be darker hours for you and me
For now there will be darker hours—just don't you give in.

The police are there to protect and serve the rich
Ticket the poor to build income for the state
Compound discrimination and disregard our rights
So don't wonder why we're so down.
Don't you worry—we won't be patronized
Someday soon we'll kick them right between the eyes

But for now there will be darker hours for you and me
For now there will be darker hours—just don't you give in.

Cities and streets will crumble, the wicked swept away
Be they just and true, eternity be thy wage.

Hoping for tomorrow, getting screwed today
All manufactured to keep us down.
But don't you worry—we won't be patronized
& someday soon we'll kick them right between the eyes.

But for now there will be darker hours for you and me
For now there will be darker hours—just don't you give in.

[Sussex Co. NJ 1995]

APPENDIX II: PROTO / BALLADS

CINDY HAS GONE FOR A BROKER

—to the tune "Johnny Has Gone for a Soldier"

O Cindy dear has gone away
so far away across the bay
my heart is tired & lonesome today
O Cindy has gone for a broker

shule shule shule agrah
there ain't no time can heal this woe
how I watched my woman go
O Cindy has gone for a broker

I'll set my clock & fix my reel
& rope them in like netted seal
& buy myself a heart of steel
O Cindy has gone for a broker

shule shule shule agrah
a man that's got no bread
is better off to stay in bed
when your love she goes for a broker

but now my tie is power red
& at the exchange I'll steal my bread
& at the exchange I'll steal my bread
O Cindy has gone for a broker

me O my I loved her so
but I was broke when she did go
but cold hard cash can heal this woe
my Cindy has gone for a broker

shule shule shule agrah
there ain't no time can heal this woe
to Standard & Poor's I'm bound to go
so Cindy can marry a broker

[Sussex Co. NJ 2001]

TAPHOUSE NEAR AN OPEN FIELD

so early in the afternoon
is nowhere to be. Birds

spring upward & a shot.
Then a draft. We go on

like that for a time. Birds
on the sill—across from

a field. We go on like
that for a time. Sitting

along the bar—birds along
the sill. So many able

bodied men out of work
so early in the afternoon.

[Pike Co. PA 2003]

CRAZY JAY (CROW JANE)

If there were such a thing
the truth of the matter
is the cops were chasing
all of us down a dead end alley.

But its much larger than
Any a one of us involved
who were sometimes cops
when we needed to be
if there were such a thing.

BATTY OLD BEN (CRAZY JANE)

Once the summer's gone
& the leaves turn brown
I hear the children playing
& draw the curtains down.

[Pike Co. PA 2003]

HERE COMES THE SUMMER
—to the tune "Buck Town Corner"

Its only when you watch
the sparrows
how they fly with speed
& accuracy

how their wings
flutter & flail in apparent
discord when they mate
that we understand
a no jest a mi a jest
nor a guess a mi a guess

the strength needed
to stay the winter
while the geese fly
awkwardly to the south.

a no jest a mi a jest
nor a guess a mi a guess

Roaming herds
of construction workers
& roofers nearly
never leave home
when autumn gold
is covered in snow.

They winter over in
warehouses like the sparrow.

la la la la la
la la la la la
la la la la la
la la la la la

They often steal away
to Buck Town Corner
ploughing snow from roads
to sing a song of summer.

[Pike Co. PA 2003]

THE PEASANT'S REPLY
—conventionally measured burden 4/4

So many curious things I saw
while walking the streets of Jersey
so many things stuck in my craw
& caused me to cringe & curse thee.

So many on the streets of Paterson
start the day with a morning drink;
things may be worse in Pakistan
but this must beg a man to think:

what despair finds solace in drink
or drugs that numb & smash
senses which writhe & fight & shrink
at a horror brought on by cash?

Come to the farmer's barren field
where absurdities grow & ripen
where the harder he works to yield
the less his annual stipend.

So you say your lonely & poor
a misfortunate overworked wretch.
Come with me & I'll show you more
of the horrors poverty can hatch.

Come to the streets of Camden Town
where Whitman used to live.
Here the children play & gun men down
for what no man can give.

Run to the well where first you heard
a lonesome child scream—
can you save her with a well-meant word
or charitable thought or dream?

So you say you know the poor
you're poor & broken too.
I warn you: throw open your door
set a table & let the rabble through.

[Sussex Co. NJ 2005]

THE BONNY MINSTREL BOY

—variation on John Hasted's Streets of London

I'm a roving blade of many a trade
& I've found work in all the trades
& if you think you know my name
you'll call me jack of all trades.

I've often heard of New York Town
the pride of this big nation
at twenty-one it's here I come
with no miscalculation.

In Brooklyn streets where I began
I found work as a martyr
but the cops & I had a falling out
that made my stay there shorter.

Then I took the train a little ways
on down to Coney Island
where I became a circus act
moonlighting as a stage hand.

In Soho Town I peddled art
in Chelsea Town a printer
but very soon they threw me out
so I became a thinker.

At NYU where I went to school
I met with a professor
who wrote a novel split an atom
& danced with a cross dresser.

On the waterfront I worked the docks
the work there it was slavery.
I tossed the job & hit the streets
& soon fell into knavery.

On Broadway Street I was a whore
on Saint Mark's Street I made songs
in every street & all streets
with my banjo I played songs

In Spanish Harlem I did have luggage
with guns & drugs—I sold it.
In Tompkins Square a liquor bottle;
I often failed to hold it.

By Brooklyn Bridge I had a bed
for all who made their way there
for intellects of great renown—
now squatters & addicts stay there.

I'm a roving blade of many a trade
& I've found work in all the trades
& if you think you know my name
you'll call me jack of all trades.

I've tried my hand at everything
from ironwork to banking
but at least I can raise my head & say
I've never been a-scabbing .

[Buffalo NY 2005]

APPENDIX III: AFTER THE BALLAD (FUTURE ANTERIOR)

TURNCOAT

Traitorous mulligrubs vault for charge
ascend into dry days tomorrow
strictly on the condition we glibly regard
today as a rite of passage—bonfires

mounted by guilt then extinguished by
the allure of what is neither labor
nor easy only to turn in the night toward
sleep on it—then come we succeed

under the occlusive stop of achievements
middling at best against this metric
shaken—to limply reload the gun if again
to repeat the traum of caving to them.

[...]

Love comes in every shade—says this ad
dissembled round the need to obscure
simple facts. Not the system of waterways
found on what Titan orbiting Saturn

but the recursive shift in art enacted by
the Olympians who crushed the
Titans when the glamor of an interest in
suffering began to spoil the party.

Love they say cuts above and beyond naïve
commitments to partisan positions but
the love we grow to love is built on a model
too graciously passed down from above.

[...]

Gripped by this fear of a career carved from
the back of a class politics the wide cast
of my lesser drives imagined an organ grinder
proletarianizing a string of marionettes

dancing like gorillas since monkeys were
spent by the libidinal force of grooming
their mates—trafficked—through the waning
of a hurricane beyond our fault but stars.

Embarking on such surrogate fantasies
segued into living by any means
necessary when the mild discomfort of
regret buckled to what advantage.

www.ingramcontent.com/pod-product-compliance
Lightning Source LLC
Chambersburg PA
CBHW051132160426
43195CB00014B/2438
* 9 7 8 0 6 1 5 9 8 3 9 3 6 *